Will Rogers Says...

Favorite Quotations
Selected by the Will Rogers Memorial Staff

Edited by
Dr. Reba Collins

Selections by Gregory N. Malak, Manager
Patricia A. Lowe, Librarian
and Dr. Reba Collins, Director Emeritus
of the Will Rogers Memorial and Research Center

Quaid Publishing LLC
Oklahoma City, Oklahoma
2008

Born November 4, 1879, in Indian Territory—near present Oologah, Oklahoma—William Penn Adair Rogers was the eighth and last child of Clement Vann and Mary America Schrimsher Rogers. Both were about one-quarter Cherokee and Will was always proud of his Cherokee heritage.

His formal schooling was sketchy, but he continued to learn throughout his life as he traveled the world in show business, dined with kings and presidents, swapped "gags" with famous writers and performers, and devoured what he read "in the papers."

Over a half-million visitors a year come to the Memorial in Claremore to see the mementoes of his life, to read some of the two million words he wrote, to view the films in which he starred and to pay tribute at his tomb. (Rogers was killed in a plane crash near Barrow, Alaska, August 15, 1935.)

Just 10 miles away on Lake Oologah is the Dog Iron Ranch—Birthplace of Will Rogers. No drug-store cowboy, Will rode and roped on the range where they ran up to 10,000 head of cattle.

Here you find the roots of his down-to-earth humor and his zest for living life to the fullest, the brilliant blue skies that were reflected in his twinkling blue eyes, and his shy charm that was as open and honest as the great Oklahoma prairie.

"Will Rogers was the greatest communicator America ever produced." So said Dr. Laurence Peter when he dedicated the Research Center at the Will Rogers Memorial in Claremore, Oklahoma, in 1982.

"Rogers excelled in every field of communication that existed during his lifetime. He was tops at the box office in his last years, the most widely read newspaper columnist, highest paid radio commentator, favorite of stage producers, a roper without peer, and everyone's favorite after-dinner speaker. No one living can measure up to that example," added the noted Peter-Principle-Man.

Staff members at the Will Rogers Memorial and Research Center readily agree. Even though we have read his writings—examined his "sayings" over and over again through the years—we still chuckle, sometimes laugh out loud as we stumble across a choice bit and suddenly see it in a new light . . . .

"Listen to this," someone will say. And we all share in wonder at his wit and his wisdom. That is why we decided to do this book. . .to share our favorite quotations with others.

Over a period of years, professional members of the Memorial staff have selected their favorites—over 2,000, all told. A committee of "readers" then made final selections for this publication.

We hope you, too, will enjoy what Will Rogers said.

Dr. Reba Collins, Director Emeritus
Will Rogers Memorial and Research Center

Contents

The Will Rogers Memorial,
Claremore, Oklahoma,
was dedicated
November 4, 1938.

What's This Country Coming To

We are not the whole of America, we are just a part of the U.S. of North America.

ML: Feb. 27, 1932

It always will seem funny to us United Staters that we are about the only ones that really know how to do everything right. I don't know how a lot of these other Nations have existed as long as they have till we could get some of our people around and show 'em really how to be Pure and Good like us.

ML: Feb. 27, 1932

Americans are getting like a Ford car—they all have the same parts, the same upholstering and all make exactly the same noises.

DTI: Oct. 20, 1926

You give us long enough to argue over something and we will bring you in proofs to show that the Ten Commandments should never be ratified.

DTII: Apr. 14, 1930

America and Russia are the only two countries left in the world with any scheme of life. Russia is trying an experiment, and America is trying everything.

DTII: Jul. 27, 1930

America has a unique record. We never lost a war and we never won a conference in our lives.

RB: Apr. 6, 1930

America is a land of opportunity and don't ever forget it.

DTIII: Jul. 1, 1931

Geography has been mighty good to us. It's wonderful to pay honor to Washington and Lincoln, but I want to tell you we ought to lay out one day a year for the old boy that laid out the location of this country. I don't know who he was, but boy he was a sage, that bird was.

RB: Apr. 6, 1930

Headlines in papers say: "Europe criticises U.S." If memory serves me right we haven't complimented them lately ourselves.

WAI: Jan. 27, 1924

YOU CAN TAKE A SOB STORY AND A STICK OF CANDY AND LEAD AMERICA RIGHT OFF INTO THE DEAD SEA.

WAI: Dec. 2, 1933

Never in our history was we as willing to blame somebody else for our troubles.

DTIV: Apr. 28, 1935

Every town should have some kind of yearly celebration. Didn't Rome have its annual bathing festival?

So think up something for your town to celebrate. Have a parade. Americans like to parade. We are a parading nation. "Upluribus paraditorious" (some paraders).

DTIII: Aug. 18, 1932

2

We don't have to worry about anything. No nation in the history of the world was ever sitting as pretty. If we want anything, all we have to do is go and buy it on credit.

DTI: Sep. 6, 1928

We are a great people to get tired of anything awful quick. We just jump from one extreme to another.

HT: Mar. 30, 1929

This country is not where it is today on account of any man. It is here on account of the big normal majority.

WAI: Feb. 22, 1925

When an Office Holder, or one that has been found out, can't think of anything to deliver a speech on, he always falls back on the good old subject, AMERICANISM.

WAI: Feb. 22, 1925

We can get hot and bothered quicker over nothing, and cool off faster than any nation in the world.

DTII: Feb. 13, 1930

Us middle class…never have to worry about having old furniture to point out to our friends. We buy it on payments and before it's paid for it's plenty antique.

DTII: Oct. 9, 1930

For the American people are a very generous people and will forgive almost any weakness, with the possible exception of stupidity.

WAI: Feb. 24, 1924

Every invention during our lifetime has been just to save time, and time is the only commodity that every American, both rich

3

and poor, has plenty of. Half our life is spent trying to find something to do with the time we have rushed through life trying to save. Two hundred years from now history will record: "America, a nation that flourished from 1900 to 1942, conceived many odd inventions for getting somewhere, but could think of nothing to do when they got there."

DTII: Apr. 28, 1930

You know no Nation has a monopoly on good things, each one has something that the others could well afford to adopt.

WAIV: Nov. 30, 1930

People are marvelous in their generosity if they just know the cause is there…

DTIII: Jun. 10, 1931

Here we go again! America is running true to form, fixing some other country's business for 'em just as we always do. We mean well, but will wind up in wrong as usual.

DTIII: Jun. 22, 1931

No nation ever had two better friends than we have. You know who they are. Well they are the Atlantic and Pacific ocean.

WAVI: Apr. 9, 1933

There is two things that tickle the fancy of our citizens, one is let him act on a committee, and the other is promise him to let him walk in a parade.
What America needs is to get more mileage out of our parades.

DTII: Sep. 1, 1929

4

My Ancestors
Dident Come Over
on the Mayflower,
but They Met 'em at the Boat

My own mother died when I was ten years old. My folks have told me that what little humor I have comes from her. I can't remember her humor but I can remember her love and understanding of me. Of course, the mother I know the most about is the mother of our little group. She has been for twenty-two years trying to raise to maturity four children, three by birth and one by marriage. While she hasn't done a good job, the poor soul has done all that mortal human could do with the material she had to work with.

RB: May 11, 1930

...Ireland. That is where some of my folks come from. There is a fine breed for you, Irish-Indian. Ziegfeld says I have a touch of Hebraic in me, too. Which would make me an Irish, Jewish, Indian.

My family crest would in that case be, a Shillalah with a Tomahawk on one end, and a percent sign (%) on the other.

WAI: Nov. 30, 1924

I am mighty happy I am going home to my own people, who know me as "Willie, Uncle Clem Rogers' boy who wouldn't go to school but just kept running around the country throwing a rope, till I think he finally got in one of them shows." They don't know how I make a living. They just know me as Uncle Clem's boy. They are my real friends and when no one else will want to hear my measly old jokes, I want to go home. It won't make no difference to them.

WAI: May 25, 1924

...I don't think I ever hurt any man's feelings by my little gags. I know I never willfully did it. When I have to do that to make a living I will quit.

WAI: Aug. 19, 1923

I am just an old country boy in a big town trying to get along. I have been eating pretty regular, and the reason I have been is because I have stayed an old country boy.

WAI: Aug. 31, 1924

Ah, folks, you can act, and talk, and do stunts, all over the world, but the applause of a home audience is sweeter to your ears than anything in the world.

DTII: Apr. 22, 1930

I think that early morning, say from seven to eight, was meant for sleeping. That's when I do all my heavy thinking—is when I am sleeping from seven to eight A.M.

ML: Feb. 27, 1932

From typewriter to linotype, Will Rogers plays the role of a small-town publisher.

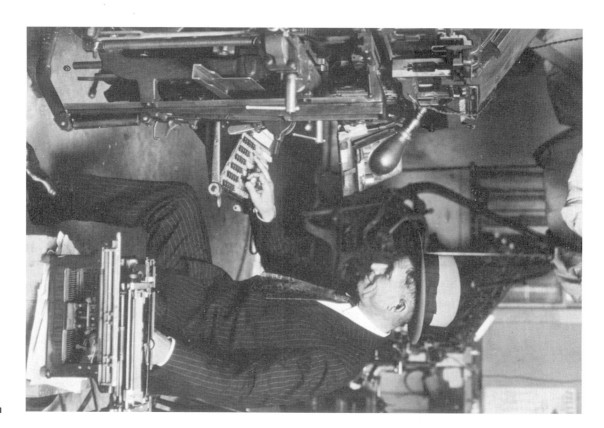

Promise Everything, Deliver Nothing

Politics and Politicians

You know the platform will always be the same, promise everything, deliver nothing.

WAIII Jul. 8, 1928

This country has gotten where it is in spite of politics, not by the aid of it.

DTIII: Nov. 1, 1932

One of the evils of democracy is you have to put up with the man you elect whether you want him or not. That's why we call it democracy.

DTIII: Nov. 7, 1932

With every public man we have elected doing comedy, I tell you I don't see much of a chance for a comedian to make a living. I am just on the verge of going to work. They can do more funny things naturally, than I can think of to do purposely.

WAI: Jan. 13, 1924

Will Rogers and Shirley Temple share honors as top box office stars in 1934.

On account of us being a democracy and run by the people, we are the only nation in the world that has to keep a government four years no matter what it does.

DTII: Feb. 21, 1930

Politics is a great character builder. You have to take a referendum to see what your convictions are for that day.

DTII May 29, 1930

That's the trouble with a Politician's life somebody is always interrupting it with an election.

WAI: unpublished

A smart state nowadays will appoint all their highway men from one place. Then one road will do all of 'em.

WAIV: Feb. 2, 1930

A Politican is just like a spoiled Kid. If he feels that his stick of candy is not the longest why he will let out a yap that will drown out the neighborhood

WAIV: Aug. 17, 1930

Lord, the money we do spend on Government. And it's not a bit better government than we got for one-third the money twenty years ago.

WAV: Mar. 27, 1932

Anyhow, how can you tell when a Vice President makes good and when he don't. They have never given one anything to do yet to find out.

CA: Jun. 13, 1932

Slogan: Be a politician; no training necessary.

WAII: Apr. 12, 1925

10

Any audience who would gather to hear a politician speak wouldn't know a good speech if they heard one.

RB: Apr. 27, 1930

There is nothing that a Vice President can do but be a Vice President. You take that title away from him and he can't hand you a Card.

HT Mar. 30, 1929

Imagine a man in public office that everybody knew where he stood. We wouldn't call him a statesman, we would call him a curiosity.

DTIII: Mar. 1, 1933

Make every speaker, as soon as he tells all he knows, sit down. That will shorten your speeches so much you will be out by lunch time every day.

CA: Jun. 28, 1924

What this country needs is more working men and fewer politicians.

WAI: Oct. 5, 1924

Never blame a legislative body for not doing something. When they do nothing, that don't hurt anybody. It's when they do something is when they become dangerous.

DTIII: Nov. 22. 1929

They say hot air rises. And I guess it does. An airplane flying over the Capitol the other day caught fire from outside sources.

WAI: Jan. 27. 1924

I wish America could get some of the political bandits that live off this country to come in and give up. Then we would know just what we were paying them to live on, instead of the present system of letting them grab what they can.

WAI: Aug. 5, 1923

A statesman is a man that can do what the politician would like to do but can't, because he is afraid of not being elected.

DTIV: Jul 5, 1934

If we could just send the same bunch of men to Washington for the good of the nation, and not for political reasons, we could have the most perfect government in the world.

WAI: Jun. 8, 1924

Politics ain't worrying this country one tenth as much as parking space.

WAI: Jan. 6, 1924

Ain't it funny how many hundreds of thousands of soldiers we can recruit with nerve. But we just can't find one politician in a million with backbone.

DTI: Feb. 18, 1929

I joke about our prominent men, but at heart I believe in 'em. I do think there is times when traces of "dumbness" crop up in official life, but not crookedness.

DTII: Mar. 18, 1930

But a politician is just like a pickpocket; it's almost impossible to get one to reform.

WAI: Mar. 25, 1923

YOU know yourself that about all there is to Politics is trading anyway.

ML: Jun. 2, 1928

In this country people don't vote for; they vote against.

RB: Jun. 9, 1935

When you straddle a thing it takes a long time to explain it.

CA: Jun. 29, 1924

They overestimate this Governor thing anyhow. States have good ones, bad ones and every kind, and yet they drag along about the same. Things in our country run in spite of government. Not by the aid of it.

DTII: Jul. 28, 1930

I am to go into Ziegfeld's new Follies, and I have no act. So I thought I will run down to Washington and get some material. Most people and actors appearing on the stage have some writer to write their material…but Congress is good enough for me. They have been writing my material for years.

WAI: Jun. 8, 1924

Once a man wants to hold a Public office he is absolutely no good for honest work.

WAII: Mar. 22, 1925

There's nothing will upset a state economic condition like a legislature. It's better to have termites in your house than the legislature.

RB: Mar. 31, 1935

Investigations

I have found out that when newspapers knock a man a lot, there is sure to be a lot of good in him.

WAL. Apr. 15, 1923

Well, what's the use of having a lot of statistics and data on something that you can't do — well, it's like garbage: What's the use of collecting it if you ain't got nowhere to put it; you don't know what to do with it. Well, that's the way with commissions.

RB: Apr. 30, 1933

You can't believe a thing you read in regard to official Statements. The minute anything happens connected with official life, why it's just like a cold night, everybody is trying to cover up.

WAII: Oct. 4, 1925

Statistics have proven that the surest way to get anything out of the public mind and never hear of it again is to have a Senate Committee appointed to look into it.

WAI: Feb. 10, 1924

They ought to pass a rule in this country in any investigations, if a man couldn't tell the truth the first time he shouldn't be allowed to try again.

WAI: Mar. 2, 1924

Presidents

A man don't any more than learn where the Ice Box is in the White House than he has to go back to being a lawyer again.

WAI: Nov. 11, 1923

Politics is the only sporting events in the world where they don't pay off for second money; a man to run second in any other event in the world it's an honor. But any time he runs second for President it's not an honor; it's a pity.

HT: Oct. 29, 1927

14

I honestly believe there is people so excited over this election that they think the President has something to do with running this country.

DTIII: Oct. 30, 1932

The high office of President of the United States has degenerated into two ordinarily fine men being goaded on by their political leeches into saying things that if they were in their right minds they wouldn't think of saying.

DTIII: Nov. 1, 1932

Harding was the most human of any of our late Presidents. There was more of the real "every day man" in him. If he had a weakness it was in trusting friends, and the man that don't do that, then there is something the matter with him sho nuff.

Betrayed by friendship is not a bad memorial to leave.

DTIII: Jun. 16, 1931

Now, if I was a President and wanted something I would claim I didn't want it. For Congress has not given any President anything that he wanted in the last 10 years. Be against anything and then he is sure to get it.

WAI: May 5, 1923

Now, take George Washington … he was a politician and a gentleman — that is a rare combination.

RB: Jun. 1, 1930

Coolidge is the first president to discover that what the American people want is to be let alone.

WAI: Jan. 27, 1924

President Franklin D. Roosevelt made a good speech yesterday and he gave aviation the biggest boost it ever had. Took his

15

family and flew out there. That will stop these big shots from thinking their lives are too important to the country to take a chance on flying.

DTIII: Jul. 3, 1932

We are a funny people. We elect our Presidents, be they Republican or Democrat, then go home and start daring 'em to make good.

DTIV: Apr. 1, 1935

We shouldn't elect a President; we should elect a magician.

DTII: May 26, 1930

The last few days I have read various addresses made on Lincoln's Birthday. Every Politician always talks about him, but none of them every imitate him.

WAI: Feb. 22, 1925

You know it's remarkable the hold that little fellow (Coolidge) has on the people. They sure do believe in him. They know that he didn't do anything when in there. But he does nothing just at the time when the people want nothing done.

WAIV: Mar. 9, 1930

Coolidge kept his mouth shut. That was such a novelty among Politicians that it just swept the Country. Funny we never had another one to think of that before. You see originality will be rewarded in any line.

WAI: Nov. 16. 1924

Being serious, or being a good fellow, has got nothing to do with running this country, if the breaks are with you, you could be a laughing hyena and still have a great administration.

DTII: Oct. 10, 1930

This would be a great time in the world for some man to come along that knew something.

DTIII: Sep. 21, 1931

I don't know who started the idea that a President must be a Politician instead of a Business man. A Politician can't run any other kind of business. So there is no reason why he can run the U.S. That's the biggest single business in the World.

WAI: Jan. 21, 1923

Congressmen and Senators

Well, you know how Congress is. They'll vote for anything if the thing they vote for will turn around and vote for them.

RB: Jun. 2, 1935

Washington, D.C. papers say: "Congress is deadlocked and can't act." I think that is the greatest blessing that could befall this country.

WAI: Jan. 27, 1924

I suggested a plan one time to shorten the Senate debate. Every time a Senator tells all he knows, make him sit down. That will shorten it. Some of them wouldn't be able to answer roll call.

RB: Apr. 27, 1930

Well, all our Senators and Congressmen are away from Washington now. This is the season of the year when they do the least damage to their country. They are scattering all over the nation. Some are going to Europe, some even to Turkey. A Senator or a Congressman will go anywhere in the world to keep from going back home and facing his people after that last Congress.

WAI: Mar. 25, 1923

You see they have two of these bodies — Senate and Congress. That is for the convenience of visitors. If there is nothing funny happening in one there is sure to be in the other, and in case one body passes a good bill, why the other can see it in time, and kill it.

WAI: Jun. 8, 1924

The Senate has furnished more officeholders and less Presidents than any industry we have.

HT: May 1, 1926

What does the Senate do with all the knowledge they demand from other people? They never seem to use it.

DTII: Jun. 12, 1930

A Senator is never as happy as when he is asking somebody a question without the party being able to ask him one back.

WAIV: Nov. 24, 1929

The things about my jokes is they don't hurt anybody. You can take 'em or leave 'em. You know what I mean. You know, you say, well they're funny, or they're terrible, or they're good, or whatever it is, but they don't do any harm. You can just pass them by. But with Congress, every time they make a joke it's a law. You know. And every time they make a law it's a joke.

RB: May 12, 1935